CW00839770

Picture credits:

U.S. GEOLOGICAL SURVEY(USGS): 29 top left, 29 top right
National Oceanic and Atmospheric Administration (NOAA): 31 bottom right
National Oceanic and Atmospheric Administration (NOAA): 34 top right, 34 bottom left
NASA/GSFC/LaRC/JPL, MISR Team: 36 top right
Norwegian Cruise Line: 42 top

Published by Robert Frederick Ltd.
4 North Parade Bath, England.
First Published: 2005

All rights reserved. No part of this publication may be reported,
stored in a retrieval system or transmitted, in any form or by any means,
electronic, mechanical, photocopying, recording, or otherwise, without
the prior permission of the copyright holder.

SEVEN WONDERS
OF THE WORLD

CONTENTS

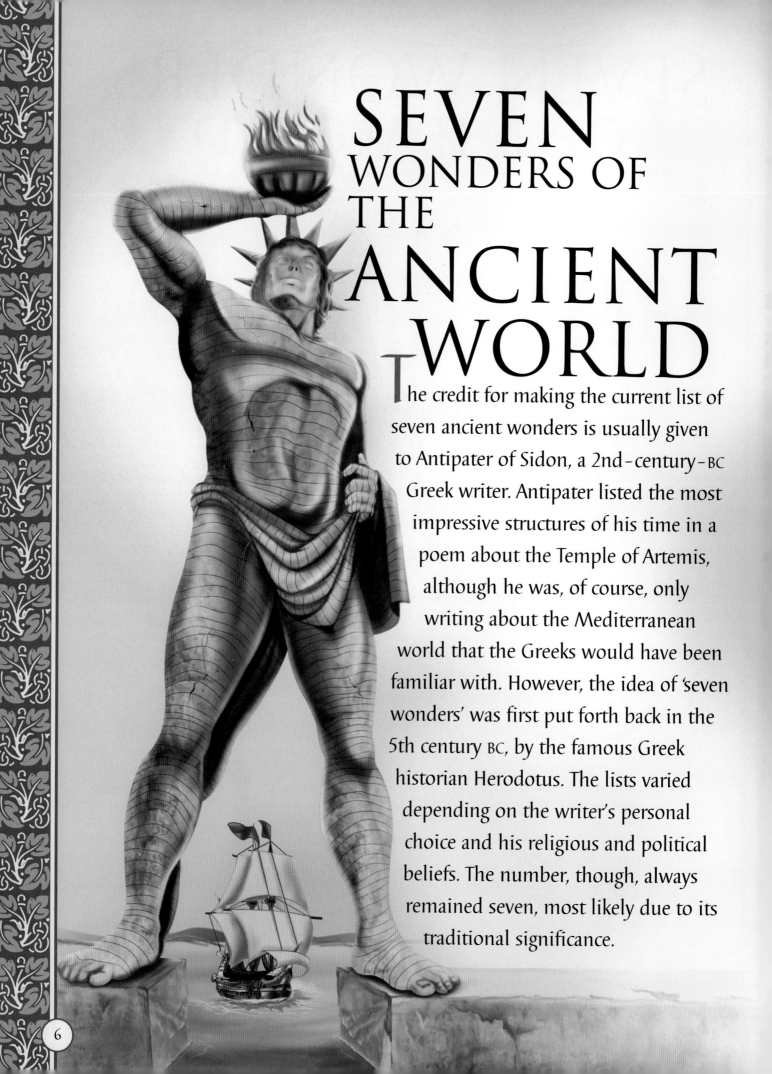

SEVEN WONDERS OF THE ANCIENT WORLD

The credit for making the current list of seven ancient wonders is usually given to Antipater of Sidon, a 2nd-century-BC Greek writer. Antipater listed the most impressive structures of his time in a poem about the Temple of Artemis, although he was, of course, only writing about the Mediterranean world that the Greeks would have been familiar with. However, the idea of 'seven wonders' was first put forth back in the 5th century BC, by the famous Greek historian Herodotus. The lists varied depending on the writer's personal choice and his religious and political beliefs. The number, though, always remained seven, most likely due to its traditional significance.

The Pyramids of Giza

The Pyramids of Giza in Egypt are a group of three pyramids and the only one of the seven ancient wonders to have survived the test of time. They are also the oldest wonders. Of the three, the largest as well as the oldest is the Great Pyramid. It was built by Khufu (Cheops in Greek), the pharaoh of the fourth dynasty.

Around AD 820, Caliph Abdullah Al Mamoun of Baghdad came to Giza. He had come in search of the fabled treasures of the Great Pyramid.

He hired a large number of workers who dug through the pyramid for weeks, with no success. Then one day, they discovered a secret passage leading to the king's chamber. However, except for an empty sarcophagus, there was nothing in there!

This was the first among several attempts to locate the treasures and remains of Khufu. What happened to the pharaoh's mummy and his treasure? The world's most amazing wonder continues to baffle even the experts.

WORD WIZARD
SARCOPHAGUS

A stone coffin, usually decorated with a sculpture, that is not buried underground. The term has been derived from the Greek name *sarkophagos*, meaning 'flesh eater'.

Location
City of Giza,
Greater Cairo, Egypt

Built
Around the year 2560 BC,
over a period of 20 years

Fact
According to Herodotus,
nearly 100,000 slaves were
used to build the
Great Pyramid!

Hanging Gardens of Babylon

It is thought that King Nebuchadnezzar II built the Hanging Gardens of Babylon for his wife, Amyitis. According to legend, Amyitis, who came from Medes, was homesick for her lush green homeland. King Nebuchadnezzar decided to cheer her up by building a garden.

All accounts of the Hanging Gardens come from Greek historians such as Strabo and Diodorus Siculus. It is believed that these were roof gardens on a series of terraces, supported by hollow pillars filled with mud so trees could be planted. The most amazing part, however, was the way the gardens were watered.

According to Strabo, buckets attached to a chain pump were used to lift water from the Euphrates River. The chain pump consisted of two wheels, one placed above the other. As these wheels turned, the buckets hung on the chain carried the river water to a pool at the top. The water was collected in the pool and later released into channels that carried it through the gardens. Nevertheless, it may be noted that most historians believe the gardens never really existed except in the minds of Strabo and Siculus!

Location
East bank of Euphrates River, near Baghdad, Iraq

Built
Reign of Nebuchadnezzar II
(Around 605–562 BC)

Fact
The name Hanging Gardens was derived from the Greek word kremastos, meaning 'overhanging'!

QUITE A WONDER!

The Terracotta Army was discovered in the tomb of the first Chinese emperor, Shi Huangdi. The army comprises more than 7,000 life-size terracotta figures of soldiers and horses. This army was buried to protect the emperor in his afterlife.

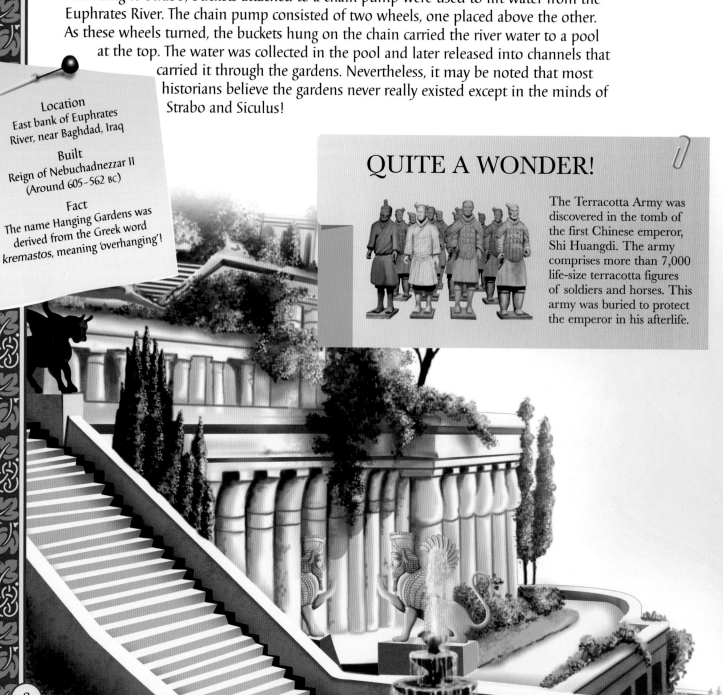

Statue of Zeus

"If Zeus moved to stand up he would unroof the temple," – so said the Greek historian, Strabo, about the Statue of Zeus at Olympia. The statue was built by the Greek sculptor Phidias.

In 456 BC, the Greek architect Libon completed the building of a magnificent temple at Olympia. This temple was dedicated to Zeus, in whose honour the Olympics were held every four years. Before the competitions, all participants paid their respects to Zeus at his temple. Although Libon's temple was a wonder in itself, the Greeks felt that it was too ordinary. So they put a statue in it.

Phidias was given the task of building the statue. He first erected a wooden frame, to which he attached plates of ivory and sheets of gold. Interestingly, his workshop was as big as the temple itself, making it possible for him to build the statue there. After carving out the various pieces separately, Phidias assembled them in the temple. However, by the time he had finished, the seated statue of Zeus almost touched the roof! That was probably why Strabo imagined that Zeus would have knocked off the roof!

Location
Ancient town of Olympia, on the west coast of Greece, about 150 km (93 miles) west of Athens

Built
Around 450 BC

Fact
The statue of Zeus was about 12 metres (40 feet) tall!

WORD WIZARD

ZEUS

The name *Zeus* has been derived from the Greek word *dios*, meaning 'bright'. Apart from being the leader of gods, Zeus was also worshipped as the god of weather.

9

Temple of Artemis

The temple dedicated to Artemis, the Greek goddess of hunting, was first built in 800 BC. Afterwards it was rebuilt several times. The one that is regarded among the Seven Wonders was built by Croesus, the king of Lydia. When Croesus invaded Ephesus in 550 BC, the temple was destroyed during the battle. Upon conquering Ephesus, Croesus offered to rebuild the temple.

The new temple was built entirely of marble. People from far and wide flocked to see this architectural marvel. The glory, however, did not last long. In 356 BC, disaster struck the temple. On the night of July 21, Herostratus, a young Greek who sought fame at all costs, burned the temple down. Legend says that on that night Artemis was too busy overseeing the birth of Alexander the Great to protect her temple.

Location
Ancient city of Ephesus,
near Izmir, Turkey

Built
Around 550 BC

Fact
After Herostratus burned the temple
down, it was rebuilt one more time.
The new temple was, however,
destroyed by Goths
in AD 262. It was never rebuilt again

QUITE A WONDER!

Machu Picchu, the 'lost city of the Incas,' is located in Peru. The name means 'old peak'. The small city was built on a mountain about 2,350 metres (7,710 feet) above the Urubamba River valley. Its ruins consist of a palace, temples and about 150 houses.

Mausoleum at Halicarnassus

There was a time when Persian kings appointed satraps (local governors) in order to rule parts of their empire. The kingdom of Caria was one such region. From 377 to 353 BC, it was ruled by King Mausolus. He made Halicarnassus (present-day Bodrum in Turkey) the capital of his kingdom.

Mausolus was married to his sister Artemisia (in those days it was common for brothers and sisters in the royal families of Caria to marry each other). Artemisia loved her husband very much. When he died, she decided to build him a memorial that would make him immortal. Hence, she ordered the construction of the mausoleum.

The tomb was made mainly of marble and decorated with larger-than-life statues of people and animals. For almost 16 centuries, it stood overlooking Halicarnassus. Later, a series of earthquakes shattered the columns and brought the roof down. In the 15th century, the Knights of Malta used the tomb's stones to build the famous crusader castle at Bodrum.

Location
City of Bodrum on the Aegean Sea, southwest Turkey

Built
Around 350 BC

Fact
The nearly 45 metres (135 feet) tall mausoleum was built on a hill and enclosed by a huge courtyard. It featured statues made by sculptors like Bryaxis, Leochares and Scopas.

WORD WIZARD

MAUSOLEUM

Today, the word 'mausoleum' is used to describe any monumental building containing a tomb. The word was derived from Mausolus and was first used to indicate the king's tomb at Halicarnassus.

11

Colossus of Rhodes

For about 56 years, the Colossus stood tall — a symbol of the courage and unity of the people of Rhodes. The magnificent statue was built in honour of Helios, the sun god. The event that led to the building of the Colossus occurred in 305 BC, more than 15 years after the death of Alexander the Great, the king of Macedonia. Antigonus, one of Alexander's generals, was the ruler of Macedonia at the time. He was upset with Rhodes for befriending his enemy, Ptolemy I Soter of Egypt. Hence, he urged his son Demetrius to invade Rhodes.

Demetrius used all his might to enter the city walls. The Rhodians, however, fought back spiritedly. Finally, Demetrius abandoned his mission. Before moving on, Demetrius left several of his war machines behind. The Rhodians melted these weapons and used the bronze to build the Colossus.

Location
At the entrance of the harbour of the Mediterranean island of Rhodes, in Greece

Built
Finished in 282 BC.
The construction took 12 years

Fact
Built by Greek architect Chares of Lindos, the Colossus was damaged in an earthquake in about 226 BC

QUITE A WONDER!

The Parthenon, dedicated to the Greek goddess Athena, was built atop the Acropolis in Athens, Greece, during the 5th century BC. The temple was decorated with several marble sculptures and it also housed a huge statue of Athena. Later, the Parthenon suffered much at the hands of invaders. While the statue of Athena was destroyed, some of the remaining sculptures were moved to the British Museum in London.

Lighthouse of Alexandria

The Pharos of Alexandria was so called after the small island it was built on. The island of Pharos lay near the coast of Alexandria and was connected to the city by a bridge. Ptolemy Soter, the Egyptian ruler of the time, realised that the sailing conditions in the region were dangerous. Hence, he ordered the construction of a lighthouse to aid ships approaching the harbour. The task was assigned to an architect named Sostratus.

According to a legend, Sostratus wanted his name inscribed on the foundation, but was not allowed to do so. Ptolemy II, Soter's son who completed the lighthouse, wanted his name carved on the structure. The clever Sostratus, however, carved his name on to the foundation and had it covered with plaster. He then inscribed Ptolemy's name into the plaster. Over the years, the plaster wore off, revealing the name of the great architect!

WORD WIZARD
PHAROS

Several variations of the word 'pharos' are now used to mean 'lighthouse'. The French phare, the Italian faro and the Portuguese farol, all have their origins in 'pharos', and mean 'lighthouse' in the respective languages!

Location
Ancient island of Pharos, Alexandria, Egypt

Built
Around 280 BC

Fact
The lighthouse is believed to have been over 134 metres (440 feet) tall. It is thought that a huge mirror, capable of reflecting the Sun's rays, was mounted atop the lighthouse

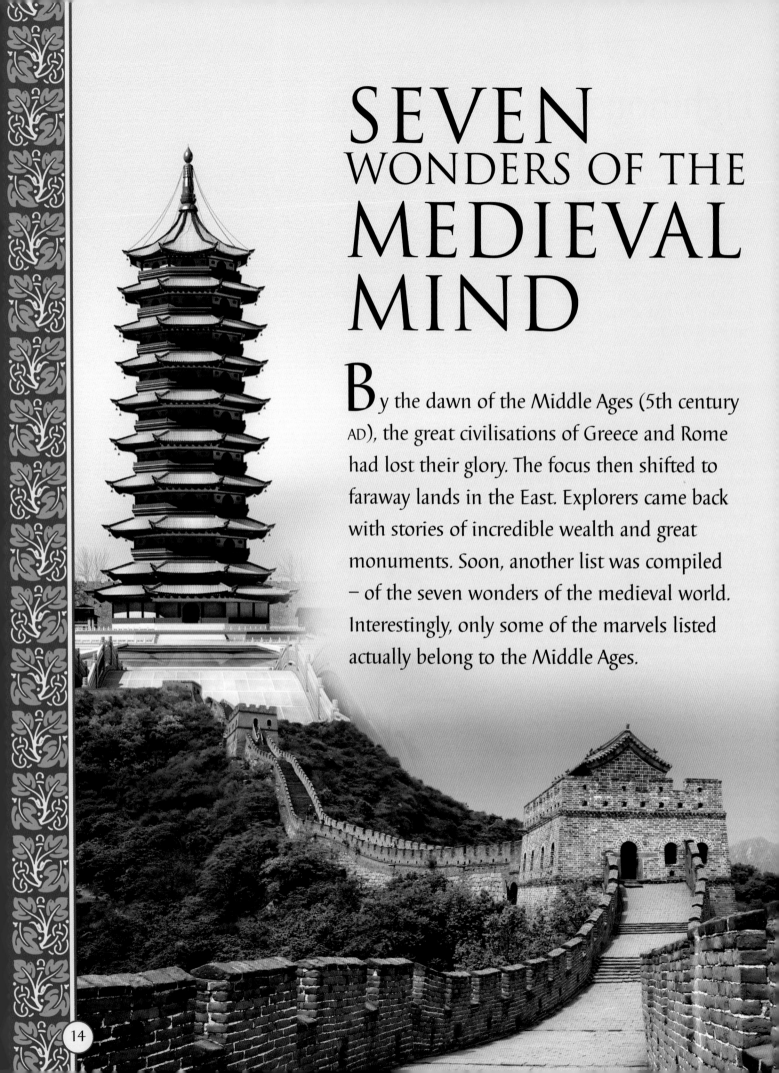

SEVEN
WONDERS OF THE
MEDIEVAL
MIND

Ꞗy the dawn of the Middle Ages (5th century AD), the great civilisations of Greece and Rome had lost their glory. The focus then shifted to faraway lands in the East. Explorers came back with stories of incredible wealth and great monuments. Soon, another list was compiled – of the seven wonders of the medieval world. Interestingly, only some of the marvels listed actually belong to the Middle Ages.

Location
About 13 km (8 miles) northwest of Salisbury, in Wiltshire, England

Built
Beginning about 3100 BC

Fact
The Stonehenge's circular bank and ditch, about 98 metres (320 feet) in diameter, were dug using antlers and animal bones!

Stonehenge

Stonehenge in Wiltshire, England, is a group of gigantic standing stones arranged in circles. The stone circles are surrounded by a large henge. It is believed that the stones were brought from faraway places. How did the ancient people transport such huge stones over long distances? No one really knows!

There are several legends regarding the origin of Stonehenge, which was probably built beginning about 3100 BC. One of the popular legends is associated with Merlin, the wizard from King Arthur's stories. It is related that in the fifth century BC, hundreds of British noblemen were killed by Hengest, a cruel Saxon leader. King Aurelianus Ambrosius wanted to build a memorial for those killed, so Merlin advised him to transport the Giants' Ring in Ireland to Britain. It was thought that giants had originally brought these stones from Africa. Merlin magically transported the stones to Britain, where they were placed around the graves of the martyrs.

WORD WIZARD

HENGE

A *henge* consists of a circular bank and a ditch, usually inside the bank. At Stonehenge, however, the ditch is located outside the bank.

Location
Rome, Italy

Built
Completed in AD 80

Fact
Some people believe that
the Colosseum got its name
from the 36-metre (120-foot)
tall bronze statue of Nero,
called Colossus Neronis, located near
the amphitheatre

Colosseum

Gladiatorial games were one of the most popular pastimes in ancient Rome. The popularity of the games inspired the Flavian emperor Vespasian to build a grand and massive amphitheatre.

The new amphitheatre could seat nearly 50,000 people! Known first as the Flavian Amphitheatre, it was renamed the Colosseum in the 8th century AD. The roughly oval-shaped Colosseum had four floors. The arena, where the contests took place, was made of wood and covered with sand. Changing rooms and animal pens were located below the arena. For over four centuries, the Colosseum served as a venue for gladiatorial games. As the games started to decline, the Colosseum was gradually allowed to fall to ruins.

QUITE A WONDER!

This symbol of eternal love was built by the Indian emperor Shah Jahan (reigned 1628-1658) in memory of his beloved wife, Mumtaz Mahal. This mausoleum of white marble was built over 22 years. Legend has it that after its completion, the architect was blinded and the hands of the sculptors chopped off, so they would not build anything to rival the beauty of the Taj!

Location
Alexandria, Egypt

Built
Second century AD

Fact
The Kom el Shoqafa's central chamber is encircled by a hallway that could hold over 250 bodies

The Catacombs of Kom el Shoqafa

This medieval wonder was discovered when a donkey fell through a hole in the ground into the chambers below. The animal had accidentally uncovered a most astonishing architectural wonder. The Catacombs of Kom el Shoqafa are located in the Egyptian city of Alexandria. They were built in the 2nd century AD for a wealthy Egyptian family that practised the ancient Egyptian religion. The catacombs were later used as a mass burial site.

A circular staircase leads into the catacombs, which consist of three levels. The main chambers include a vestibule and a central tomb chamber. To the left of the vestibule was a funeral banquet hall. There, friends and relatives of the dead held feasts in the person's memory. The tomb chamber was decorated with sculptures of the Egyptian gods Horus, Thoth and Anubis – all of which were carved in the Greco-Roman style.

WORD WIZARD

CATACOMB

An underground burial place with passages, consisting of holes in the walls to hold the bodies. The word has been derived from the Greek term *kata kumbas*, meaning 'near the low place.'

17

The Porcelain Tower of Nanjing

The breathtaking Porcelain Tower at Nanjing, China, was built by the Chinese emperor Yung-lo in his mother's honour. According to legend, a small pagoda containing a statue of Buddha had stood on the site for more than 1,000 years, before the Porcelain Tower was built. The pagoda was destroyed during a war. As a tribute to the site, Yung-lo chose to raise his new pagoda there. The construction of the tower began in 1413.

The outer walls of the pagoda were covered with white porcelain bricks. Each of the nine floors had overhanging eaves made of glazed green porcelain tiles. Hundreds of bells and lanterns were hung from the eaves, making the structure an unforgettable sight. The tower later suffered much destruction during warfare.

QUITE A WONDER!

The temple of Angkor Wat is located in Angkor, Cambodia. Built by the Khmer king Suryavarman II, the temple was dedicated to Vishnu, the Hindu god. An outstanding feature of the temple are the slightly raised stone sculptures that run along the outer walls, narrating various stories from Hindu mythology.

Location
On the banks of the Yangtze, Nanjing, China

Built
Beginning 1413

Fact
The Chinese referred to the Porcelain Tower as Bao'ensi, which means 'Temple of Gratitude.' The tower rose to a height of about 80 metres (260 feet)

The Great Wall of China

Called 'Wan-Li Qang Qeng' in Chinese, the Great Wall was originally a number of separate walls built to keep invaders out. It was in 214 BC that Shi Huangdi, the first Chinese emperor, undertook to join the separate sections.

Several legends are attached to the Great Wall. One such is related to King You of the Western Zhou Dynasty. The king's wife, Baosi, was known to never smile. The king promised to reward the person who could make the queen smile. A cunning official named Guo Shifu suggested setting fire to the watchtower of the wall. He said that this would fool the army and make the queen smile at the trick.

King You followed Shifu's advice, and sure enough, the queen burst into laughter, seeing the troops rush to the border. But alas – the king repeated his little prank once too often! In 771 BC, enemies invaded Western Zhou. Once again, the watchtower was set on fire. This time, however, no one came to help the king, who was killed by the invaders.

WORD WIZARD

WAN-LI QANG-QENG

The Chinese word means *10,000 Li Long Wall*. A value of 10,000 Li is equal to about 5,000 kilometres (3,107 miles).

Location
Across the mountains of northern China, winding to the north and northwest of Beijing, the capital

Built
Emperor Shi Huangdi joined the various parts in the 3rd century BC

Fact
The Great Wall of China covers a distance of more than 6,700 km (4,163 miles)!

Leaning Tower of Pisa

It was not meant to lean! When construction of the world's most famous bell tower began in 1173, the architect had designed it to be vertical. So imagine his horror when he first noticed the lean. However, it is this unusual feature that makes the Leaning Tower of Pisa, in Italy, one of the wonders of the world.

The tower was built on soft soil. As the weight of the tower increased, one side started to sink – causing the tower to lean. Work was stopped immediately. When construction resumed in about mid-13th century, architects strived to adjust the lean, but failed. Over the years, several attempts have been made to control the lean. In 1998, experts removed soil from the other side of the tower to correct the imbalance as far as was possible, and prevent it from collapsing.

Location
Pisa, Italy

Built
Construction began in August 1173

Fact
Built over a span of nearly 200 years, the Leaning Tower is about 55 metres (180 feet) tall

QUITE A WONDER!

It was Easter Sunday in the year 1722. The Dutch explorer Jacob Roggeveen and his crew sighted a strange island. Roggeveen was curious and decided to explore. As they neared the island, the Dutch crew was dumbstruck by the sight that greeted them.

The coastline was dotted with gigantic faces carved out of rocks. Roggeveen named his discovery Easter Island.

Location
Istanbul, Turkey

Built
Rebuilt in its present form between 532 and 537 by Emperor Justinian I

Fact
Originally called Megala Ekklessia ('Great Church'), the Hagia Sophia was turned into a museum in 1934 by the orders of Kemal Atatürk, the founder of the Turkish Republic

Hagia Sophia

The Hagia Sophia in Istanbul, Turkey, is undoubtedly the finest example of Byzantine architecture. The original cathedral was built by the Roman emperor Constantius II, son of Constantine I the Great – who founded the city of Istanbul (then called Constantinople, and still earlier, Byzantium) and made it his capital. After the first church was destroyed by a rioting mob in AD 404, Emperor Theodosius II built a second church on the same site. This was burnt down during the Nika revolt of 532. The present building was built in 532–537 during the reign of the Byzantine emperor Justinian I.

WORD WIZARD

HAGIA SOPHIA

The name *Hagia Sophia* is Greek for 'sacred wisdom'. Holy Wisdom is one of the attributes traditionally associated with Jesus Christ.

The Hagia Sophia's dome was the most unique aspect of the church. Forty windows formed the base of the dome, giving the illusion that it floated over the church.

A series of severe earthquakes caused much of the dome to fall apart in 558, and it was replaced with a smaller version by 563. The Hagia Sophia was converted into a mosque when the Ottoman Turks captured Constantinople in 1453. During the Ottoman rule, minarets were built around the church and the interior of the church was redecorated to resemble a mosque. Today, the Hagia Sophia serves as a museum of Byzantine art.

21

SEVEN
WONDERS OF THE
NATURAL
WORLD

Y ou have seen how amazing manmade wonders can be. Yet, these marvels pale before the wonders of Mother Nature, painstakingly created over millions of years. Nothing we can build or shape can ever be as majestic or as awesome as those spectacles created by the world around us. The wonders listed here will simply take your breath away!

Location
On the border between
Nepal and Tibet

Fact
The mountain was named after the British surveyor general of India, Sir George Everest, who first produced detailed maps of the Himalayas. Since Hillary and Norgay conquered the peak, around 1,500 people have repeated the feat.

Mount Everest

"Because it's there." – This was how George Mallory, a famous British mountain climber, replied when a reporter asked him why he wanted to climb Mount Everest. On June 8, 1924, Mallory and fellow Englishman Andrew Irvine set off to conquer the world's tallest summit. Unfortunately, neither of them survived.

At an estimated 8,850 metres (29,035 feet), Mount Everest is not only the tallest mountain but also one of the most difficult ones to climb. It belongs to a mountain chain called the Himalayas, and is located on the border between Nepal and Tibet. Mount Everest was first identified as the world's tallest mountain in 1852. Ever since, it has attracted many climbers who aspire to reach its summit. All those early attempts failed.

Then, on May 29, 1953, two men braved the forces of nature to achieve what seemed impossible. On that historical day, Edmund Hillary of New Zealand and Tenzing Norgay, his Nepalese partner, looked down at the world from the highest peak.

WORD WIZARD
MOUNT EVEREST

In Nepal, Mount Everest is known as *Sagarmatha*, meaning 'Forehead of the Sky.' The Tibetans call it *Qomolangma*, which means 'Mother of the Universe.'

Location
Colorado Plateau in
northern Arizona

Fact
The Grand Canyon is about 446 km
(277 miles) long and roughly 1.6 km
(one mile) deep. It is made up of
layers of rock, each older than the
one above it. The oldest layer was
formed about two billion years ago!

Grand Canyon

It was September 1540. Captain García López de Cárdenas, a Spanish explorer, arrived in Arizona, U.S., in search of the legendary treasures of the seven cities of Cibola. Cárdenas and his men did not find the fabled cities, but they did find a natural treasure – the Grand Canyon! Cárdenas became the first European to sight the wonder.

A canyon is a deep valley flanked by cliffs on either side, formed by rivers or streams and years of erosion. The Grand Canyon was formed by the Colorado River cutting a channel in the course of hundreds of millions of years, and also by erosion. Scientists believe the region was covered by sea all those millions of years ago. Gradually, the land was pushed up above the sea level forming a high flatland – in other words, a plateau. In time, a river started to run through the plateau. Slowly, the river cut into the rocks to form the massive canyon.

QUITE A WONDER!

The aborigines of Australia call it Uluru. According to them, Uluru was once under an ocean. A great battle took place on its shores, in which thousands died. Saddened by the bloodshed, the ocean threw up a huge blood-coloured rock – the Uluru! Whatever the story, the oval-shaped Ayers Rock in the Simpson Desert, Australia, has the distinction of being one of the largest monoliths (large block of stone) in the world.

Nile River

WORD WIZARD

NILE

The Nile gets its name from the Greek word *Neilos*, meaning 'river valley.' Ancient Egyptians used to call it *iteru*, which simply means 'river'.

Egypt is known as the 'gift of the Nile' – and why not? One of the world's greatest civilisations flourished on the banks of the River Nile. If it had not been for this great river, Egypt would not have flourished at all! The Nile is the world's longest river. It has two main tributaries – White Nile and Blue Nile. The White Nile starts from Lake Victoria in Uganda, while the Blue Nile begins at Lake Tana in Ethiopia. The two meet at Khartoum, the capital of the Sudan, to form the Nile.

In ancient times, the Nile used to flood every year, depositing fertile black soil on its banks. This soil was excellent for agriculture and soon people settled on the riverbank. Even today, a majority of the Egyptian population live on the banks of the Nile. The construction of the Aswan Dam has stopped the annual flooding. The floodwater is now stored for cultivating crops as well as for producing electricity.

Location
Africa

Fact
The Nile travels through nine countries before joining the Mediterranean Sea. Apart from agriculture, ancient Egyptians also used the Nile for transport and trade. The Nile is over 6,650 km (4,132 miles) long

Victoria Falls

The Victoria Falls is considered to be the world's largest curtain of water. The locals call it 'Mosi-oa-Tunya', meaning 'the smoke that thunders.' This is an apt name since the falls looks like rising smoke when viewed from air. The falls are located on the Zambezi River, between Zambia and Zimbabwe. They are composed of six separate falls divided by islands on the Zambezi.

The Scottish explorer David Livingstone was the first European to discover the falls. He first laid eyes on them on November 16, 1855. He named the falls after Queen Victoria. In his diary, Livingstone wrote, "…scenes so lovely must have been gazed upon by angels in their flight." No one has since been able to describe the breathtaking beauty of the falls better.

Location
On the Zambezi River, which at this point forms the border between Zambia and Zimbabwe

Fact
The height of the falls range from 90 metres (295 feet) to 105 metres (344 feet). The falls include Devil's Cataract, Rainbow Falls, Horseshoe Falls, Eastern Cataract, Main Falls and Armchair Falls

QUITE A WONDER!

Mount Kilimanjaro is a volcanic mountain in Tanzania, Africa. With a central cone, Kibo, rising to a height of about 5,895 metres (19,340 feet), Kilimanjaro is the highest mountain in Africa. Its name in Swahili means 'the mountain that glitters.' Although Kilimanjaro has not erupted in recent times, its youngest cone, again Kibo, continues to emit steam.

Location
Southeastern Brazil

Fact
Apart from the view it offers, Corcovado is also famous for the statue of Christ the Redeemer. The 30-metre (99-foot) tall statue was built in the first half of the 20th century.

Harbour of Rio de Janeiro

On New Year's Day in 1502, Portuguese explorers sailing down Brazil's coast arrived at a narrow opening in the coastline, with mountains on either side. As they passed through the entrance, the explorers saw a huge body of water. Thinking that they had discovered the mouth of an unknown river, the Portuguese named it River of the First of January. And that's how Rio de Janeiro (capital of Brazil in 1822–1960) got its name!

The body of water that the Portuguese had seen was, in fact, a bay. The locals called it Guanabara, meaning 'arm of the sea.' The former Brazilian capital is located on the west side of the bay. One of the mountains that guarded the bay entrance is called Sugar Loaf Mountain, probably after the shape of the mould used to refine sugar cane. The other mountain, the Corcovado, is 710 metres (2,329 feet) high and offers a bird's-eye view of the harbour. The locals are so proud of their city that they say, "God made the world in six days and on the seventh He concentrated on Rio."

WORD WIZARD

RIO DE JANEIRO

Rio de Janeiro in Portuguese means 'River of January', while Corcovado means 'hunchback'. The mountain was so named because its profile seemed hunched over!

Northern Lights

The northern lights are a spectacular display of lights over the Northern Hemisphere. The scientific name for this phenomenon is *aurora borealis*.

The northern lights are, in fact, the visible effect of the solar wind, which is a stream of electrically charged particles emitted by the Sun. These particles travel at an average speed of 800 kilometres/second (500 miles/second) and reach the Earth in about two or three days.

If it passes the Earth's atmosphere, solar wind has the power to destroy life on the planet. However, the magnetic field around Earth prevents this from happening. The solar wind also carries magnetic particles. Hence, even as it comes into contact with the Earth's magnetic field, the particles repel each other.

In this cosmic battle, the Earth's North and South poles attract some of the solar particles. As they move towards the poles, the particles collide with the atoms and molecules of the upper atmosphere there. These movements become visible when the particles clash with atmospheric gases like oxygen and nitrogen, creating splashes of colour in the sky.

QUITE A WONDER!

Niagara Falls is located on the Niagara River, between the United States and Canada. It consists of three separate falls – Horseshoe Falls, American Falls and Bridal Veil Falls. More than 14 million tourists visit the falls every year!

Location
The aurorae appear over the Earth's polar regions in what are termed as the auroral ovals – these usually extend over Finland, Scandinavia, Canada, the northern United States, Alaska and Siberia

Fact
Aurora is the Roman goddess of the dawn, while *borealis* is from Boreas, the Greek god of the northern wind

Parícutin Volcano

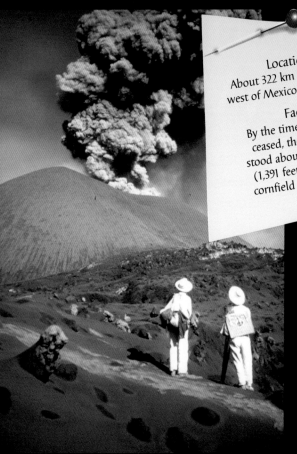

Location
About 322 km (200 miles)
west of Mexico City, Mexico

Fact
By the time eruptions
ceased, the Parícutin
stood about 424 metres
(1,391 feet) above the
cornfield it rose from.

On February 20, 1943, Dionisio Pulido, a Mexican farmer from Michoacán, was working his fields as usual. Suddenly, Pulido felt the ground beneath tremble. As he stood watching, a 46-metre- (150-foot)-long fissure opened up and began to emit smoke. Within 24 hours, the volcano had grown to about 50 metres (164 feet) in height and had started to throw up pyroclastic rocks. By March, volcanic activity intensified. People from the nearby towns of Parícutin and San Juan were evacuated. By August that year, the towns were almost totally buried under layers of lava and ash.

The volcano was extremely violent during the first year of its growth. Within the year, it was over 336 metres (1,100 feet) tall. It continued to erupt for the next eight years, before finally becoming quiet in 1952. The Parícutin gained significance also because it provided scientists the rare chance to study the lifecycle of a volcano from its birth through growth, until its death!

WORD WIZARD

PYROCLASTIC

Pyroclastic rocks are fragments of magma (or molten rock) thrown into the air during violent volcanic eruptions. The term 'pyroclastic' comes from the Greek words *pyro* ('fire') and *klastos* ('broken').

SEVEN
WONDERS OF THE
UNDERWATER
WORLD

Water bodies such as lakes, rivers and oceans hold some
of the most beautiful and intriguing sights in the world.
Man's interest in the distinct environment of the deep seas
has become keener with time – seen especially in the growing
popularity of diving as a sport. Hence, it was decided that a
list exclusively dedicated to underwater wonders would be
appropriate. It was also felt that such a list would help protect
and create awareness about the fragile marine environment.

Palau

It is considered a diver's paradise. This small archipelago in the Pacific Ocean is said to hold some of the richest coral reefs in the world. Scientists have identified 700 species of corals and about 1,400 species of fish in the waters around Palau. The coral reefs are home to cuttlefish, giant clams, brittle stars, sharks and rays, among others.

Millions of years ago, coral polyps (small creatures that build coral reefs) began to colonise the underwater volcanoes in the region. These tiny creatures built hard skeletons of limestone around their soft bodies for protection. As the corals died, new ones continued to build skeletons. Gradually, these coral-topped mountains were raised above the water. The exposed corals died, but new ones continued to build homes on the slopes underwater.

Palau also boasts 80 marine lakes, the most popular being the Jellyfish Lake. Remember the jellyfish forest in the movie *Finding Nemo*? Well, you can see a real-life jellyfish forest at the Jellyfish Lake! Unlike the jellyfish in the movie, though, the yellow, polka-dotted jellyfish of Palau are harmless.

WORD WIZARD
ARCHIPELAGO

The term *'archipelago'* is the collective name for a group of several islands usually spread in the open sea.

Location
An independent country in the Pacific Ocean, Oceania

Fact
Palau comprises about 340 coral and volcanic islands. A species of colourful giant clams, called *Tridacna Crocea*, is found naturally only in Palau

31

Galapagos Islands

In 1835, a ship named HMS *Beagle* arrived at the Galapagos Islands. On board was a young naturalist named Charles Darwin. The young scientist was struck by the fact that the finches and tortoises he found on the various islands were different from each other. He collected a few specimens for further study.

About 24 years later, Darwin published his revolutionary book, *On the Origin of Species* (1859). It contained Darwin's famous theory of evolution and also explained the concept of 'survival of the fittest'. Maybe if it had not been for the Galapagos Islands, one of the most important scientific discoveries would never have been made!

The islands continue to be home to several rare species of birds and animals. They are best known for the giant tortoises found there. Marine iguanas, sea lions, penguins and about 19 known types of seabirds also live among the Galapagos Islands.

Location
In the Pacific Ocean, about 1,000 km (621 miles) west of the coast of South America

Fact
The Galapagos Islands comprise 13 major volcanic islands and several smaller islands. Various species of sharks, like the Galapagos sharks and the giant whale sharks, swim the waters around the islands

QUITE A WONDER!

Krakatoa is a volcano that was located on the Indonesian island of Rakata. In August 1883, the volcano erupted causing a large part of Rakata to disappear. Tsunamis caused by the eruption destroyed about 165 villages and killed over 36,000 people.

Belize Barrier Reef

"The most remarkable reef in the West Indies," is how Charles Darwin described the Belize Barrier Reef. At over 290 kilometres (180 miles), this barrier reef is the second longest of its kind in the world.

Belize is known not only for its spectacular barrier reef, though. It also boasts of three offshore atolls. Normally, atolls form atop undersea volcanoes. The three atolls in Belize, however, have been formed on non-volcanic mountains under the ocean. These atolls are known as Lighthouse Reef, Glover's Reef and Turneffe.

The Lighthouse Reef is famous for its crater, the Blue Hole. This crater leads to what was a dry cave during the Ice Age. When the ice melted, sea levels rose and flooded the cave. The roof of the cave collapsed leaving behind the Blue Hole. Stalactites formed during the Ice Age can still be seen deep inside the hole.

WORD WIZARD
STALACTITE

A stalactite is a column of rock that hangs from the roof of a limestone cave. It is formed over a long period of time, by water drops containing lime. The term has been derived from the Greek word *stalaktos*, meaning 'dripping'.

Location
Extends 220 km (137 miles) from the Belize/Mexican border in the north to the Sapodilla Cayes in the south

Fact
The reef shelters about 65 species of corals and over 500 kinds of marine animals. The Blue Hole is about 300 metres (1,000 feet) in diameter and over 120 metres (400 feet) deep

Northern Red Sea

Ras Muhammad, a coral plateau in the Northern Red Sea, is often called the ocean's 'Garden of Eden'. The name seems to be justified, since the plateau is filled with soft corals in yellow, orange and green, and a variety of hard corals. Sea anemones, clownfish, triggerfish, bright-red lionfish and friendly Napoleon wrasses complete the picture.

Ras Muhammad is also one of the world's most popular sites for wreck diving. Among the wrecks are *Dunraven*, a British steamer that sank in 1878; *Thistlegorm*, a World War II supply ship; and *Yolanda*, a Cypriot ship that went down in 1980. The *Dunraven* was once thought to be on a secret mission for Lawrence of Arabia when she sank, though this has since been disproved. The *Yolanda* site is unusual – while the ship itself has plunged into the deep sea, its cargo of toilet bowls can be found scattered along the reef!

Location
The Red Sea is located along the east coast of Egypt

Fact
Some strange pieces of cargo that can be found in the Ras Muhammad diving site include ammunition shells, motorcycles and even a railroad car!

QUITE A WONDER!

The Blue Grotto is a unique cave in the island of Capri, Italy. The sunlight, passing through tiny underwater openings, illuminates the sea from below. This fills the cave with its magical blue colour. Ancient Roman statues adorn a landing place inside the cave, adding to its beauty.

Location
Siberia, near the
Mongolian border

Fact
Lake Baikal is 636 km
(395 miles) long and
1,620 metres (5,315 feet) deep.
It is said that it would take a
whole year for all the rivers
of the world combined
to fill Lake Baikal!

Lake Baikal

It is the oldest existing freshwater lake on our planet. Lake Baikal is also the deepest lake, containing more water than all of North America's Great Lakes combined! The lake stays covered with ice for part of the year.

WORD WIZARD

ENDEMIC

The word 'endemic', when used with regard to plants and animals, means 'native to a certain region.' Such plants and animals are not found anywhere else except in that particular region.

The Sacred Lake, as Lake Baikal is known among the Russians, is situated in southeast Siberia. It is surrounded by the Barguzin Mountains as well as various forests. The lake supports more endemic species than any other lake in the world. It contains about 50 different species of fish, including sturgeon and the famous omul salmon.

One of the most interesting animals that lives there is the Baikal seal, or nurpa. It is the world's only freshwater seal. During winters, when the ice begins to form, the nurpas carve out elaborate dens using their sharp claws. A distinct feature of these dens are their long tunnels and canopies, which are wonders in themselves.

Location
In the Coral Sea, off the coast of Queensland in northeast Australia

Fact
The Great Barrier Reef is approximately 2,012 km (1,250 miles) long. The reef, like the Great Wall of China, can be seen from outer space!

Great Barrier Reef

The Great Barrier Reef is not just the world's longest coral reef, but it is also the largest natural structure on Earth built by living organisms. The reef is situated in the Coral Sea, stretching from Queensland to Bundaberg in Australia.

The Great Barrier Reef consists of a network of about 2,800 distinct reefs and some 900 islands. It harbours nearly 2,000 species of fish — a number that is increasing with the discovery of new species every year. About 350 types of reef-building corals, 250 species of shrimps and 4,000 kinds of molluscs also reside there. Further, the reef is known for its wide range of sharks including grey reef sharks and silvertips.

QUITE A WONDER!

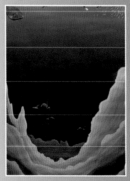

With a depth of about 10,911 metres (35,800 feet), the Challenger Deep stands out as the deepest point in the ocean. It is located in the Mariana Trench, near the island of Guam in the Pacific Ocean. The point is named after the British survey ship that discovered the area in 1951 — the HMS *Challenger II*. On January 23, 1960, the U.S. Navy submersible *Trieste* became the first manned vessel to touch the bottom of the point.

Deep-Sea Vents

In 1977, marine scientists Richard Lutz and Peter Rona set off in the submersible *Alvin* to help shoot a movie, *Volcanoes of the Deep Sea*. As they reached the ocean depths, it became pitch dark and the water was extremely cold. No living forms, except for a few strange-looking creatures that glowed, could survive in such conditions. As *Alvin* approached an underwater mountain range, the scientists saw black smoke rising from huge chimney-like structures. Amazingly, creatures like tubeworms, shrimps and fish surrounded these 'chimneys'. The scientists had discovered what we know to be deep-sea hydrothermal vents!

Hydrothermal vents are found in regions of high volcanic activity. The water in these regions seeps into the Earth's surface through cracks on the ocean floor. This water is heated by the surrounding magma. When the water becomes extremely hot, it rises through the vents. This hot water is rich in minerals and chemicals. Some of the minerals are deposited around the vent to form the chimney-like structures that Lutz and Rona saw.

WORD WIZARD

SUBMERSIBLE

A *submersible* is a small submarine-like vessel usually operated in the ocean depths, with little use at the surface. It is especially used in a range of research, rescue and salvage operations.

Location
In deep seas, specifically in regions of intense volcanic activity

Fact
The water in deep-sea vents can be as hot as 400ºC (750ºF). When the hot water mixes with the cold seawater, the minerals in the hot water are precipitated (formed into particles). This makes the vent water appear black. Hence, the name 'black smoker'!

SEVEN
WONDERS OF THE
MODERN
WORLD

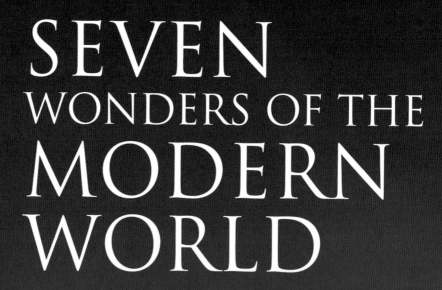

The list of Seven Wonders of the Modern World was compiled by the American Society of Civil Engineers (ASCE). These were judged on factors like design, construction, importance to humanity, and engineering challenges overcome during construction. Since a proposed project had to be a completed one for it to be considered a modern wonder at the time, several structures that were built later could not be included. This ensures that soon there will be another list – of 'seven wonders of the 21st century!'

Empire State Building

It took just one year and 45 days to complete this architectural wonder of modern times!
Today, the Empire State Building is one of the most recognised structures across the world and a cherished symbol of the spirit of New York, U.S. It was built in 1930 during the Great Depression. By this time, skyscrapers had become popular in the United States. People were competing with each other to see who could build the tallest skyscraper.

In New York the competition was between two powerful industrialists, Walter Chrysler (commissioned the Chrysler Building) and John Jakob Raskob (Empire State Building).

The nearly 443 metres (1454 feet) tall Empire State Building was constructed at an average rate of four and a half floors per week! Construction workers laboured even on Sundays and holidays to hurry the process. Finally, all the hard work paid off when, on May 1, 1931, the Empire State Building officially overtook the Chrysler Building as the tallest skyscraper in the world!

Location
350 Fifth Avenue, New York

Built
1930–1931

Fact
The Empire State Building has 102 floors. The spire on the building serves as a lightning rod to the surrounding area, diverting the lightning into the ground through a wire

WORD WIZARD

GREAT DEPRESSION

The *Great Depression* refers to the period between 1929 and 1934, when the world, especially the United States, faced one of its biggest economic slumps ever. The period was marked by mass unemployment and poverty.

CN Tower

It all started due to bad television signals. In the 1960s, the tall skyscrapers of Toronto, Canada, hindered proper transmission of signals. It was at this point that the Canadian National Railway Company (CN) decided to step in and save the day. The organisation proposed to build a transmission tower that would be taller than all of Toronto's skyscrapers. The result was the CN Tower – the tallest freestanding structure in the world!

The tower has four observation levels including the Sky Pod, the world's highest manmade observation deck at 447 metres (1,467 feet). The Glass Floor and the Outdoor Observation deck are located at a height of 342 metres (1,122 feet), while the Indoor Observation deck stands at 346 metres (1,136 feet). Another popular feature of the tower is the 360 Restaurant located about 351 metres (1,150 feet) above ground. The restaurant rotates once every 72 minutes, providing a complete view of the city below.

QUITE A WONDER!

Located in Keystone, South Dakota, U.S., the Mount Rushmore National Memorial was sculpted to represent the first 150 years of independent America. The famous American sculptor Gutzon Borglum and some 400 workers sculpted the busts of George Washington, Thomas Jefferson, Theodore Roosevelt and Abraham Lincoln – each about 18 metres (60 feet) tall – over a period of nearly 14 years!

Location
Toronto, Ontario
province, Canada

Built
1976

Fact
The CN Tower is 553 metres (1,815 feet) tall. More than two million tourists visit the tower every year

Location
In the Paraná region in Brazil, close to the Brazil-Paraguay border

Built
1975-1991

Fact
The Itaipú Dam is 196 metres (643 feet) tall. This hydroelectric dam is a joint venture between Brazil and Paraguay, and meets their power-supply needs to a large extent

Itaipú Dam

The biggest challenge that faced the engineers of the Itaipú Dam was shifting the course of the world's seventh largest river. They spent almost three years on digging a diversion channel for the Paraná River! After removing about 50 million tons of mud and creating a 2-kilometre (1.3-mile) long diversion channel, the workers were finally able to start work on the dam.

The Itaipú Dam is a gravity dam. Hence, it had to be massive and strong. There is only one material that could meet this requirement — concrete. However, the engineers of Itaipú Dam chose a hollow gravity structure that required much less concrete than a normal gravity dam. Despite the use of less concrete, the dam is as sturdy as any other gravity dam in the world.

WORD WIZARD

GRAVITY DAM

A *gravity dam* is an extremely heavy structure that controls the water with its weight

Location
Panama, between the
Atlantic and Pacific oceans

Built
1904–1914

Fact
The Panama Canal is 82 km
(51 miles) long. The largest ships that
can pass through the canal locks of
the Panama Canal are classified as
Panamax

Panama Canal

King Charles I of Spain was the first to propose a canal through the Isthmus of Panama, back in the 16th century. However, over three centuries passed by before construction was begun – by the French! After working on the canal for 20 years, the French gave up due to financial problems. Eventually, in 1903, the United States undertook the task of building the canal.

The Panama Canal connects the Atlantic and Pacific oceans. The most interesting feature of the canal are its canal locks – two sets on the Pacific side and one on the Atlantic side. Canal locks are devices that lift or lower ships and boats from one water level to another. They are used in regions where there is a drastic difference in water levels – as is the case with the Panama Canal, where the Pacific end is higher than the Atlantic end. Small railway engines haul the ships through the locks. The Panama Canal was opened on August 15, 1914.

QUITE A WONDER!

The Suez Canal connects the Mediterranean Sea with the Red Sea. It offers a direct route from Europe to Asia, without going around Africa. Except for supertankers, all large ships can navigate this 163-kilometre (101-mile) long canal and today around 50 ships cross the canal daily.

Channel Tunnel

In 1984, when the governments of England and France called for proposals to build a railway link between the two countries, it was not the first time that the idea was mooted. This time, though, the dream was to become a reality, in the form of the Channel Tunnel, also known as the Eurotunnel. Construction began in 1988 and it took 15,000 workers over seven years to complete the tunnel.

The Channel Tunnel consists of three tunnels – two for rail traffic and a smaller service tunnel in between. The service tunnel acts as an escape route in case of fires. The most difficult part of the construction was boring a tunnel through the soft, chalky seabed of the English Channel. Huge tunnel-boring machines were used for the purpose. At the same time, a concrete liner was used to coat the permeable tunnel walls and prevent the sea from flooding the tunnel. Boring was carried out simultaneously from both the English and the French sides. The tunnel was officially opened on May 6, 1994.

Location
Beneath the English Channel at the Straits of Dover, connecting Cheriton in Kent, England, and Sangatte, France

Built
1988-1994

Fact
The Channel Tunnel is 50 km (31 miles) long, of which about 39 km (24 miles) is undersea

WORD WIZARD

PERMEABLE

A *permeable* surface is one that allows liquids or gases to pass through it.

Golden Gate Bridge

Building the Golden Gate Bridge was a mammoth task in the 1930s. The bridge connects San Francisco to Marin County in California, U.S. The region is well known for its strong winds, fogs and earthquakes. Despite the odds, the enterprising engineer Joseph Strauss was confident that his design would withstand both the forces of nature and the test of time.

First, the towers were set up. The north pier supporting the tower was built on a solid rock layer. The pier on the San Francisco side posed a special challenge, though. The engineers had to build it in the open ocean, about 343 metres (1,125 feet) from the shore and 30 metres (100 feet) below the water.

Once the towers were completed, the cables were slung from them. Completed in a little over four years, the historical Golden Gate Bridge opened to the public in 1937. Today, it is one of the most recognised structures in the world.

Location
Between San Francisco and Marin counties, California, U.S.

Built
1933–1937

Fact
The steel wires used in the cables of the Golden Gate Bridge are long enough to circle the earth three times! The twin towers are more than 227 metres (746 feet) high

QUITE A WONDER!

The Eiffel Tower, named after its builder Gustave Eiffel, is the most recognised structure in the Paris skyline. The 300-metre (984-foot) tall tower was built in 1889 to celebrate 100 years of the French Revolution. It was the world's tallest structure until 1930, when Chrysler Building in New York City took over.

Location
The Netherlands

Built
Completed in 1986

Fact
The final storm-surge barrier of the North Sea Protection Works was erected in 1997 near Rotterdam

North Sea Protection Works

This is the story of a nation's fight against the wrath of the mighty sea. For years, the Netherlands had to suffer the consequences of being located below sea level. This contributed heavily to many disastrous floods that caused huge losses of lives and property. In 1916, one particularly destructive flood hit the areas near the estuary once known as Zuiderzee. The Dutch government sprung into action and decided to dam the Zuiderzee. The construction of a 30-kilometre- (19-mile)-long dyke was begun.

The project proved good enough to protect the northern provinces from another major storm in 1953. Unfortunately, though, the southwestern provinces – near the delta formed by the Meuse and Rhine rivers – suffered grave damages. This resulted in the so-called Delta Project. It included the 2.8-kilometre (1.75-mile) long Eastern Schelde barrier, one of the most sophisticated storm barriers ever built. This moveable barrier comprises concrete piers and steel gates that are dropped only during storms. Together, these projects form one of the biggest wonders in engineering – the North Sea Protection Works.

WORD WIZARD

ESTUARY

An *estuary* is the wide part of a river that enters the sea. Here, the freshwater mixes with the salt water. A delta is formed when soil is deposited at the mouth of a river. A river delta is formed at the place where the river enters the sea.

SEVEN WONDERS LEGEND

ANCIENT WONDERS:

1. The Pyramids of Giza
2. Hanging Gardens of Babylon
3. Statue of Zeus
4. Temple of Artemis
5. Mausoleum at Halicarnassus
6. Colossus of Rhodes
7. Lighthouse of Alexandria

MEDIEVAL WONDERS:

1. Stonehenge
2. Colosseum
3. The Catacombs of Kom el Shoqafa
4. The Porcelain Tower of Nanjing
5. The Great Wall of China
6. Leaning Tower of Pisa
7. Hagia Sophia

NATURAL WONDERS:

1. Mount Everest
2. Grand Canyon
3. Nile River
4. Victoria Falls
5. Harbour of Rio de Janeiro
6. Northern Lights
7. Parícutin Volcano